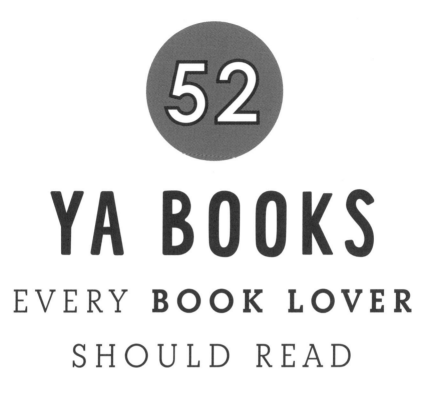

52

YA BOOKS

EVERY **BOOK LOVER**

SHOULD READ

A ONE-YEAR JOURNAL

and Recommended Reading List from
the American Library Association

ALAAmericanLibraryAssociation

The fifty-two titles featured in this book were selected by editors at the American Library Association and the reviews come from *Booklist*. *Booklist* is the book review magazine of the American Library Association and is a vibrant source of reading recommendations for all readers. It's been considered an essential collection development and readers' advisory tool by thousands of librarians for more than 100 years. For more information, visit booklistonline.com. To read *The Booklist Reader*, *Booklist*'s blog for book lovers, visit booklistreader.com.

Published by Sourcebooks
P.O. Box 4410, Naperville, Illinois 60567-4410
(630) 961-3900
sourcebooks.com

Printed and bound in the United States of America.
VP 10 9 8 7 6 5 4 3 2 1

CONTENTS

INTRODUCTION

Welcome, dear reader!

As an avid reader and lover of library books, you are in for a treat with this collection. This one-year reading journey invites you to explore a full listing of must-read young adult (YA) titles selected by the American Library Association.

The goal is not just to complete each title but also to relish the journey. Here's what you can expect: each week, you will be introduced to a fresh new title to read and cross off your list. A short write-up and review from the ALA will whet your appetite for the work, and a writing prompt is paired with each title so you can explore your thoughts as you read. The selected titles span genres, from fantasy and graphic novels to nonfiction and more, and all are reader favorites within the YA category!

With fun extras throughout, including additional book trackers, this journal is a book club in your hands...and a reading adventure to savor.

Are you ready to read?

MY ALL-TIME
FAVORITE BOOKS

A place to track everything else I'm reading

READING LOG

Titles completed and everything else I am reading

DATE STARTED	TITLE	DATE COMPLETED

DATE STARTED	TITLE	DATE COMPLETED

The Poet X

ELIZABETH ACEVEDO

This story from the streets of Harlem centers on Xiomara Batista, a teenage poet seeking to express herself. X has loved writing down her thoughts from an early age. Unfortunately, she doesn't get to share them with her family, due to her mother's strict dedication to making sure X is focused on being a good Catholic girl. When X starts questioning her faith and realizes her brother is hiding his own secrets from their mother, she starts figuring out how she can stand up for herself and her beliefs. This is a powerful, heartwarming tale of a girl not afraid to reach out and figure out her place in the world.

Describe a time when you stayed silent and wished you hadn't. How can you speak up in your own life?

Kit's Wilderness

DAVID ALMOND

Thirteen-year-old Kit Watson and his family have returned to the English coal-mining town of Stoneygate to care for Kit's recently widowed grandfather. Almost immediately, Kit is enticed by John Askew, also of an old mining family, into a game called Death. Like the other members of Askew's gang, Kit is left alone in an abandoned mine until he sees ghosts of ancestors who died there as boys. Kit's friend Allie tells him that the other kids pretend to see these appari-tions, but Kit really does see—and Askew knows it. The boys share a bond. Both are artistic: Kit is a writer; Askew is an artist. And both are sensitive enough to perceive what may not be there. But Kit comes from a strong, loving family, and Askew is the child of an ineffectual mother and a father who's a vicious drunk. Slowly, as Kit hears sto-ries from his grandfather and writes his own, he realizes he has a mission—to save John Askew, body and soul.

Stories play an important role in this book. What stories does your family tell?

Speak: The Graphic Novel

LAURIE HALSE ANDERSON,
ILLUSTRATED BY EMILY CARROLL

Melinda, a high school freshman, is dealing with the traumatic aftermath of rape. Not only is Melinda trying to forget her rape—a challenge when her rapist freely wanders the halls of their school—she's flailing in her classes and is an outcast among her peers until an art-class assignment and some slow-building friendships give her the courage to speak up. The artwork in this graphic novel—an adaption of Anderson's groundbreaking original prose novel—features creeping, smudgy shadows; faces with missing eyes and mouths; and jagged panel borders. It captures the acute terror of Melinda's rape, the pernicious paranoia that follows her in its wake, the swirling rumors and bullying surrounding her, and glimmering moments of hope and comfort.

When have you felt powerless in your life? How did you regain your power?

Symphony for the City of the Dead: Dmitri Shostakovich and the Siege of Leningrad

M. T. ANDERSON

Dmitri Shostakovich was witness to an almost overwhelming number of changes and transformations in his native Russia. From the rise of Communism under Lenin to Stalin's Great Terror and, perhaps most monumentally, the Siege of Leningrad, the Russian composer was there, often drawn dangerously close to the clutches of Stalin's seemingly random rage. All the while, he defiantly wrote moving, galvanizing music. This nonfiction book interweaves details from Shostakovich's life with pivotal historical moments, particularly Russia's role in World War II, brilliantly elucidating some of the more puzzling parts of Russian history. This is a captivating account of a genius composer and the brutal, stormy period in which he lived.

What role does music play in your life? What would your life be like without music?

DATE STARTED:

DATE FINISHED:

MY RATING:

☆ ☆ ☆ ☆ ☆

Damsel

ELANA K. ARNOLD

A prince ventures into the wilderness to slay a dragon and save a damsel. When he returns home with his rescued bride, he becomes king. That is how it has been in the kingdom of Harding and how it will always be. Sound familiar? Perhaps, but it's not how this story ends. The first thing Ama knows is waking up in Prince Emory's arms as they ride toward his home. "I saved you," he tells her, and though she has no memory of the thing he saved her from, she believes him. In his castle, as their wedding approaches, she learns to become the perfect queen: calm, obedient, gentle. Ama works at becoming small, but flashes of memory are starting to return to her, and there is more in this castle—and in her heart—than can be contained.

What are some ways you can be bolder in your life?

DATE STARTED:

DATE FINISHED:

MY RATING:

☆ ☆ ☆ ☆ ☆

Ship Breaker

PAOLO BACIGALUPI

In a world in which society has stratified, fossil fuels have been consumed, and the seas have risen and drowned coastal cities, Nailer, age seventeen, scavenges beached tankers for scrap metals on the Gulf Coast. Every day, he tries to "make quota" and avoid his violent, drug-addicted father. After he discovers a modern clipper ship washed up on the beach, Nailer thinks his fortune is made, but then he discovers a survivor trapped in the wreckage—the "swank" daughter of a shipping company owner. Should he slit the girl's throat and sell her for parts or take a chance and help her? This is a vivid, brutal, and captivating story.

Who did you help today? Who helped you?

52 YA Books Every Book Lover Should Read

Lovely War

JULIE BERRY

It's 1942, and a stylish couple can barely keep their hands off each other as they take an elevator up to their hotel room—where the woman's husband awaits. But this is no ordinary trio. They are revealed to be the Greek gods Aphrodite, Ares, and Hephaestus, Aphrodite's long-suffering husband, the god of forges and fire, who entraps the adulterers in a gold mesh net. Aphrodite tells Hephaestus he knows nothing of love, but she can show him what it looks like. Aphrodite takes the whole night to spin a story that wraps her relationship with Ares, the god of war, around the story of four lovers who meet during World War I: James Alderidge, on his way to the front; Hazel Windicott, a pianist who has a few days to fall in love with him; Colette Fournier, a young Belgian woman whose family has all been killed by the Germans; and Aubrey Edwards, a Black soldier who is in France to both play jazz with an infantry band and fight for America.

Greek gods have extraordinarily interesting personalities and roles within Greek mythology. Which one are you most like?

Going Bovine

LIBBA BRAY

Cameron, a sixteen-year-old C-plus-average slacker who likens himself to "driftwood," suddenly becomes the center of attention after he is diagnosed with Creutzfeldt-Jakob disease, the human form of mad cow disease. In the hospital, he meets Dulcie, an alluring angel clad in fishnet stockings and combat boots, who presents him with a heroic quest to rescue the planet from an otherworldly, evil force. Guided by random signs and accompanied by a teen dwarf named Gonzo, Cameron sets off on a wild road trip across the United States to save the world, and perhaps his own life. Talking yard gnomes, quantum physics, cults of happiness, mythology, religion, time travel, the blues, Disney World, the vacuous machine behind reality TV shows, and spring break's beer-and-bikini culture all figure prominently in the plot in this dark comedy.

What would you do if you knew there wouldn't be any consequences?

A Heart in a Body in the World

DEB CALETTI

A guy in a parking lot leers at her, and Annabelle Agnelli takes off running. Eleven miles later she stops, only to realize that running is exactly what she needs to do. Not just an impromptu, panic-stricken bolt, but an outlandishly extreme run that will take her from Seattle to Washington, DC. It might help with her PTSD, and it might help her come to terms with her body. It will surely give her time to mourn the terrible losses of the previous year and atone for the role she never meant to play. Annabelle was on the rebound from a disrupted relationship when she befriended a socially awkward boy, now known only as "The Taker." Annabelle couldn't decide if he was weird or cute and tried not to encourage him, but looking back, she is tormented by her every smile and kindness.

If you were going through a tough time, what sort of activity would you immerse yourself in to feel better? Why/how would it help you?

Stolen

LUCY CHRISTOPHER

Drugged and kidnapped from her parents at the Bangkok airport, English teen Gemma wakes to find herself in the weirdly beautiful but desolate Australian outback. Her only company is her captor, a handsome young Australian named Ty, who is obsessed with her. Indeed, he tells her that he has been watching her since she was a child and now plans to keep her with him forever. Told in the form of a letter Gemma is writing to Ty, this novel is a complex psychological study that is also a tribute to the hypnotic beauty of the outback, which Ty passionately loves and feels has been "stolen" by those who would exploit it for gain. Though Gemma at first hates both her kidnapper and the landscape, she gradually begins to warm toward both.

Describe a time when you felt an unexpected connection to a person or place.

Little & Lion

BRANDY COLBERT

Suzette's back in California for the summer after spending the year at boarding school in New England, and she's looking forward to being home, though she's nervous about reuniting with her step-brother, Lion. Before she left for school, she broke a promise to Lion and told their parents his bipolar disorder was getting out of control. Now that she's back, she's worried she irrevocably altered their relationship, and while she's trying to rebuild it, Lion starts to spiral again. Meanwhile, Suzette is facing some new truths about herself too. At boarding school, she was surprised to fall hard for her roommate, Iris, and back home, she's even more surprised to discover feelings for her old friend Emil, her mother's best friend's son. As the summer unfolds, Suzette learns to navigate key elements of her identity—Black, Jewish, bisexual—in a world that seems to want her to be only one thing.

What are the key elements of your identity?

The Ropemaker

PETER DICKINSON

According to legend, a powerful magician has isolated the Valley for eighteen years to protect it from the armies of the Empire in the south and the fierce, marauding horsemen of the north. But now something is terribly wrong. Young Tilja sets out with her grandmother Meena, the boy Tahl, Tahl's grandfather, and an ill-spirited horse on a daunting quest to find the magician in hopes he will renew the magic that protects the Valley. Their trek through the tightly controlled Empire is fraught with danger. Along the way, Tilja discovers her extraordinary power, a power that connects her to the Ropemaker, a mysterious being who appears along the route in many guises. It's left to Tilja and the Ropemaker to make things right in both the Valley and the Empire.

Describe your extraordinary power.

Little Brother

CORY DOCTOROW

Seventeen-year-old techno-geek "w1n5t0n" (a.k.a. Marcus) bypasses the school's gait-recognition system by placing pebbles in his shoes, chats secretly with friends on his IMParanoid messaging program, and routinely evades school security with his laptop, cell, WiFinder, and ingenuity. While skipping school, Marcus is caught near the site of a terrorist attack on San Francisco and held by the Department of Homeland Security for six days of intensive interrogation. After his release, he vows to use his skills to fight back against an increasingly frightening system of surveillance. Marcus prepares to stage a techno-revolution. Though it's set in the near future, this tense, fast-paced sci-fi adventure may seem, at times, frighteningly familiar.

Do you feel that the connectedness of modern technology is a benefit or a threat to our society?

52 YA Books Every Book Lover Should Read

The House of the Scorpion

NANCY FARMER

Young Matteo (Matt) Alacrán is a clone of the original Matteo Alacrán, known as El Patrón, the 142-year-old absolute ruler of Opium, a country separating the United States and Aztlan, once known as Mexico. In Opium, mind-controlled slaves care for fields of poppies, and clones are universally despised. Matt, on El Patrón's orders, is the only clone whose intelligence has not been blunted. While still quite young, Matt is taken from the loving care of El Patrón's cook and placed into the abusive hands of a maid who treats him like an animal. At seven, brought to El Patrón's attention, he begins an indulged life, getting an education and musical training, though he is never allowed to forget that he is not considered human. At fourteen, Matt learns that El Patrón has had other clones who have provided hearts and other organs so El Patrón can go on living. What will happen to Matt?

Have you stood up for something you believe in? What was it, and why did you take a stand?

Looking for Alaska

JOHN GREEN

Sixteen-year-old Miles Halter leaves his boring life in Florida in hopes of boarding school adventures in Alabama. A collector of famous last words, Miles is after what the dying François Rabelais called "the Great Perhaps." At the boarding school, he is blessed with a fast-talking and quick-witted roommate who just so happens to be friends with the enigmatic and beautiful Alaska Young. It's Alaska who introduces Miles to the purported last words of Simón Bolívar: "Damn it. How will I ever get out of this labyrinth?" It is a question that haunts Miles as he and his friends are forced to cope with loss.

What is your life motto?

Ordinary Hazards

NIKKI GRIMES

This memoir from Nikki Grimes is told in the form of a powerful and inspiring collection of poems. She details her early life through adulthood, and she unabashedly explores the highs as well as the lows. Grimes's struggles with a mother suffering from mental illness, an absent father, and an abusive stepfather plunged her life into turmoil at an early age. Yet through it all, she persevered and used writing as an outlet for her pain. She delves into finding a loving family after being separated from her older sister and bounced around in foster care, ultimately having to choose between her found family and her birth mother. She writes about love, family, responsibility, belonging, finding your place in the world, and fighting the monsters you know—and the ones you don't.

In what ways do you think keeping a diary, journal, or blog could move your life forward in a new direction?

Seraphina

RACHEL HARTMAN

After forty years of peace between human and dragon kingdoms, their much-maligned treaty is on the verge of collapse. Tensions are already high with an influx of dragons, reluctantly shifted to human forms, arriving for their ruler Ardmagar Comonot's anniversary. But when Prince Rufus is found murdered in the fashion of dragons—that is, his head has been bitten off—things reach a fever pitch. Seraphina, a gifted court musician, wants only to go unnoticed as the investigation draws close: she is the unthinkable, half human and half dragon, and her secret must be protected. But when Prince Lucian Kiggs asks for her help with the murder investigation, she has no choice but to become involved, even if Kiggs's acute perceptiveness is a danger to her.

Describe the most courageous thing you have ever done.

Charles and Emma:
The Darwins' Leap of Faith

DEBORAH HEILIGMAN

When this book opens, Charles Darwin is trying to make a decision, and he is doing so in time-honored fashion: drawing a line down a piece of paper and putting the pros of marriage on one side and the cons on the other. As much as Darwin is interested in wedded life, he is afraid that a family will take him away from the revolutionary work he is doing on the evolution of species. However, the pluses triumph, and he finds the perfect mate in his first cousin Emma, who becomes his comforter, editor, mother of his ten children—and sparring partner. Although they got along well, Charles and Emma were on opposite sides when it came to the role of God in creation. This book uses Darwin family letters and papers to show the personal influences that shaped Charles's life as he worked mightily to shape his theories.

What is one thing you've always wanted to learn more about?

DATE STARTED:

DATE FINISHED:

MY RATING:

☆ ☆ ☆ ☆ ☆

We Are the Ants

SHAUN DAVID HUTCHINSON

Self-hating teenager Henry is caught in an existential trap. Finding life to be absurd, he thinks humans are not the apex of civilization—on the contrary, they are no more significant than ants. Are they even worth saving? A relevant question, for Henry has a secret: the aliens who have abducted him a dozen times or more have told him when the world will end. Strangely, they have also given him the choice to prevent doomsday; he can simply press a button, and the world will live on. Yet will he take that action? His boyfriend, Jesse, has committed suicide, and Henry, blaming himself, doubts that life is worth living. Certainly, his is a grand parade of suffering and humiliation (because of his belief in aliens, he is called "space boy" at school). But then charismatic Diego shows up in town, and suddenly life has renewed purpose. But does Henry really have the freedom of choice he thinks he has?

Think of a major decision you've faced and chronicle it here.

52 YA Books Every Book Lover Should Read

Allegedly

TIFFANY D. JACKSON

Mary B. Addison was nine when a jury quickly convicted her of a crime the public was already convinced she'd committed: the murder of Alyssa Richardson, a white infant that African American Mary and her mother were babysitting. Back then, Mary kept quiet about the incident. Now almost sixteen, she has spent the better part of her life under lock and key, first in "baby jail" and then in a group home. But Mary has a boyfriend now, and they're expecting a baby, and there's no way the state will let a convicted baby killer keep her child. For the first time since her trial, Mary may actually have to speak about her childhood, her tumultuous relationship with her mother, and what happened—allegedly—that night.

What secrets do you keep? What would happen if you shared them?

21

We Are the Perfect Girl

ARIEL KAPLAN

Aphra Brown has a smart mouth, a big nose, and a best friend she'd die for: Bethany. To the casual observer, Bethany is Aphra's opposite: painfully shy where Aphra is vibrant and funny, and a stunning classic beauty where Aphra is, as some might put it, strong-featured. Bethany is head over heels for Greg D'Agostino, an admittedly great guy—Aphra once had a crush on him herself. But Bethany, of course, is too shy to ever do anything about it. When a class project goes horribly wrong, Aphra pretends to be an advice-giving AI for a few late-night class chats. Greg figures out that the class-project AI is a real person fast enough, but when he gets the mistaken impression that the girl behind the curtain is Bethany and asks her out in real life, Aphra, unwilling to stand in the way of Bethany's happiness and not trusting that Greg would be thrilled to know it was her and not her beautiful friend, doesn't say a word. But Bethany, still shy, struggles to connect with Greg and is desperate for Aphra's help. And Aphra's keeping too many secrets.

Have you ever chosen a friend's happiness over your own? Was it the right decision?

DATE STARTED:

DATE FINISHED:

MY RATING:

☆ ☆ ☆ ☆ ☆

22

I Crawl Through It

A. S. KING

Four seniors try to escape personal traumas in the face of daily bomb threats at their high school. But who is behind the threats? The four teens aim to find out. At the center of the story is Stanzi, a biology genius who feels split in two and is forced on family "vacations" to sites of school shootings: "I own the most morbid snow globe collection in the world." She is in love with Gustav, a physics genius (natch) busy building an invisible helicopter. China Knowles, meanwhile, has swallowed herself after a terrible experience with her boyfriend, becoming a "walking digestive system." And Lansdale Cruise is a beautiful, pathological liar with long hair that grows like Pinocchio's nose.

How do you "crawl through" tough days and times when you feel like you just might explode?

52 YA Books Every Book Lover Should Read

Hey, Kiddo

JARRETT J. KROSOCZKA, ILLUSTRATED BY THE AUTHOR

In this graphic memoir, Jarrett Krosoczka recounts his sometimes troubled childhood, spent largely with his grandparents; his struggle to maintain a relationship with his heroin-addicted mother; and his gradually developing love for making art and comics. His grandparents officially took custody of Krosoczka when he was not yet five years old, and it wasn't until much later that he learned about his mother's heroin addiction and imprisonment. Life with his grandparents—a hard-drinking couple who bickered constantly—wasn't always easy, but his grandfather was a stalwart supporter of his artistic aspirations, and he slowly realized that the atypical family he ultimately collected (even eventually his father, whom he finally met late in his teen years) could be enough.

Who is your biggest supporter? How do they support you?

We Are Okay

NINA LACOUR

It's the winter break during Marin's first year at college, and she is facing the holidays thousands of miles from her San Francisco home. Since her grandfather died the previous summer, Marin feels set adrift. Not only has she lost Gramps, her sole caretaker, but he'd been keeping secrets, and when she discovers the truth, it shatters everything she believed was true about her life. Engulfed in pain and feeling alone, she shuns her best friend Mabel's numerous calls and texts. But Mabel flies cross-country, determined to help her friend deal with her grief. Marin is afraid that Mabel regrets the physical intimacy that had grown between the two girls while she was still in California and braces herself for more heartache, but Mabel surprises her in more ways than one.

Describe a time when you experienced a loss.

Butterfly Yellow

THANHHÀ LẠI

Eighteen-year-old Vietnamese refugee Hằng carries several secrets as she makes the perilous journey to family in Texas. One: in the waning days of the war, Hằng handed over her five-year-old brother, Linh, at an airlift. Almost immediately, the eleven-year-old realized her plan for both of them to be taken, with her unknowing parents to somehow follow, was stupid. Now, years after being separated from her brother, Hằng arrives in Texas, eager to reclaim her relationship with the little boy she remembers. In a madcap adventure that includes a bus ride and bizarre travel arrangements with an aspiring young cowboy, Hằng makes her way to Linh, now David, only to discover that he has no recollection of her or his old life in Vietnam and has no desire to reacquaint himself with her. Can Hằng find a way to reconnect with her brother and help him remember details about their life in Vietnam?

What parts of your past would you like to make peace with?

52 YA Books Every Book Lover Should Read

26

The Disreputable History of Frankie Landau-Banks

E. LOCKHART

In the summer between her freshman and sophomore years, Frankie Landau-Banks transforms from "a scrawny, awkward child" with frizzy hair to a curvy beauty, "all while sitting quietly in a suburban hammock, reading the short stories of Dorothy Parker and drinking lemonade." On her return to Alabaster Prep, her elite boarding school, she attracts the attention of gorgeous Matthew, who draws her into his circle of popular seniors. Then Frankie learns that Matthew is a member of the Loyal Order of the Basset Hounds, an all-male Alabaster secret society to which Frankie's dad had once belonged. Excluded from belonging to or even discussing the Bassets, Frankie engineers her own guerilla membership by assuming a false online identity.

Have you ever felt excluded from a group? What did you do about it?

All the Wind in the World

SAMANTHA MABRY

Lakes have dried up, the earth is dying, and Sarah Jac and James flee southwest, leaving behind a gritty Chicago to harvest maguey in the desert. Surrounded by other transient workers, they hoard their money, hiding their love and scamming other workers while they dream of a different future. After an accident forces them to flee, the two find themselves working at the Real Marvelous, a ranch that's rumored to be cursed. The owner of the ranch has two daughters, and Sarah Jac, who knows her way around a horse, is asked to give the youngest, timid and angry Bell, riding lessons. At the same time, James catches the eye of the eldest, fierce and beautiful Farrah, ill with a mysterious terminal disease. As Sarah Jac and James are inexorably drawn into this family and their secrets, strange and magical things begin to happen at the Real Marvelous—things no con in the world can overcome, things that even their love may not be able to withstand.

Describe a relationship of yours that wasn't what it seemed.

The Earth, My Butt, and Other Big Round Things

CAROLYN MACKLER

Fifteen-year-old Virginia Shreves is the blond, round, average daughter in a family of dark-haired, thin superstars. Her best friend has moved away, and she's on the fringes at her private Manhattan school. She wants a boyfriend, but she settles for Froggy Welsh, who comes over on Mondays to grope her. Virginia tries to lose weight, struggles with her "imperfections," but she just can't seem to catch up with her perfect siblings. She especially idolizes her older brother, Byron, who's a natural athlete, handsome, and wildly popular. So when he's accused of raping a classmate and is kicked out of college, she has to come to terms with her "perfect" family and its secrets.

What "imperfections" do you struggle with?

A Very Large Expanse of Sea

TAHEREH MAFI

Jaded and cynical in the face of repeated cruelty at the sight of her hijab, Shirin only plans to get through high school as quickly as she can and let no one past her guarded exterior. It works until she meets Ocean James, who sees more than just her headscarf and is charmingly persistent about learning who she is, from her love of music to her burgeoning skills on the break-dancing team her brother starts. But while Ocean's presence is a breath of fresh air, it also terrifies her: What happens when he gets past her walls? What happens when they shatter and she's left more vulnerable than ever before?

Have you ever judged someone too quickly? What did you miss out on as a result?

Jellicoe Road

MELINA MARCHETTA

Taylor Markham isn't just one of the new student leaders of her boarding school; she's also the heir to the Underground Community, one of three battling school factions in her small Australian community (the others being the Cadets and the Townies). For a generation, these three camps have fought "the territory wars," a deadly serious negotiation of land and property rife with surprise attacks, diplomatic immunities, and physical violence. Only this year, it's complicated: Taylor might just have a thing for Cadet leader Jonah, and Jonah might just be the key to unlocking the secret identity of Taylor's mother, who abandoned her when she was eleven.

What is the hardest part of being a leader?

The White Darkness

GERALDINE McCAUGHREAN

Fourteen-year-old Symone's only friend is an imaginary incarnation of Captain Lawrence "Titus" Oates, an explorer who accompanied Robert Scott on his failed expedition to the South Pole. Sym is passionate about the Antarctic, and her infatuation is fed by Uncle Victor, an eccentric family friend who has cared for Sym and her mother since Sym's father's death. When Victor surprises Sym with a trip to "the Ice," she has some doubts, especially when she discovers that her mother can't come. But her excitement overshadows her initial misgivings—until she realizes that Uncle Victor has an obsession of his own that runs deeper than the glaciers and threatens her life.

Describe a time when you felt that someone was out to get you. What did you do to stop them?

I, Claudia

MARY McCOY

Imperial Day Academy, an elite prep school in Los Angeles, has teachers, administrators, and an elected student senate. But the true power at Imperial Day lies in the honor council, an elected group of students that uphold the school's strict honor code. Claudia is a self-proclaimed outsider. With chronic health problems and an oft-mocked stutter, her proximity to power comes only from her benevolent older sister's honor council position. But Claudia is also a student of history, and as she recounts the corrupt reigns of a string of honor council presidents for an unnamed jury, the reader will begin to realize that her years of studying political machines have turned Claudia into one herself.

Would power corrupt you? Why or why not?

Blood Water Paint

JOY McCULLOUGH

This novel in verse follows the heartbreaking but inspiring true story of gifted Roman painter Artemisia Gentileschi. Raised since she was twelve solely by her volatile, abusive, and less talented artist father, Artemisia spends her days as her father's apprentice, grinding pigments and completing most of his commissions. At first, she thinks she has found solace with her charming new painting instructor, Agostino Tassi, who awakens a dormant passion in her, but slowly she grows to fear him as he asserts control over her and ultimately rapes her. Her mother's stories of bold, ancient Roman heroines guide Artemisia through her harrowing trials with Tassi, show her how to paint her truth, and eventually inspire most of her iconic paintings.

How do you cope with difficult emotions?

Dumplin'

JULIE MURPHY

Willowdean Dickson, self-proclaimed fat girl and Dolly Parton enthusiast, has this to say: "The word *fat* makes people uncomfortable." Will's mother (who calls her Dumplin') is a former winner of the local Miss Teen Blue Bonnet contest and now runs it, which makes pageant season an unwelcome constant in Will's life. To ignore it, she concentrates on her friendship with her bestie, Ellen, and her crush on fellow fast-food worker Bo, while trying to shake her grief over the death of her beloved 498-pound aunt. Knowing what it means to be fat, as well as what it means to her mother to be thin, Will decides to be happy being herself. Because why not? But when Bo kisses her behind the dumpster, and she and Ellen flame out, her life is turned inside out, and who she is becomes a question more than an answer.

Think of someone you admire, respect, or find "invincible."
What do you like best about this person?

----

52 YA Books Every Book Lover Should Read

I'll Give You the Sun

JANDY NELSON

When Noah's mom suggests that he and his twin sister, Jude, apply to a prestigious arts high school, he is elated, but Jude starts simmering with jealousy when it becomes clear that their mother favors Noah's work. Noah soaks up the praise, though a little callously, happy to hone his painting skills and focus on the guy across the street, who could be more than a friend. Fast-forward three years, and everything is in pieces. Their mother has died in a car crash, and Noah, who wasn't accepted into the art school, has given up painting, while Jude, who was accepted but is no longer the shimmering, confident girl she once was, is struggling in her sculpture class. All her clay forms shatter in the kiln; is her mother's ghost the culprit? Determined to make a piece that her mother can't ruin, Jude seeks out the mentorship of a fiery stone carver (and his alluring model, Oscar).

How does art influence you?

Airborn

KENNETH OPPEL

Matt Cruse is a cabin boy aboard the luxury passenger airship *Aurora* when the ship encounters a battered hot air balloon with an unconscious man aboard. Before dying, the man claims to have seen beautiful creatures swarming in the air over an uncharted island. Not until a year later, when Matt meets the man's granddaughter, Kate de Vries, who boards the *Aurora*, does he learn that the man wasn't hallucinating. Pirates board, rob, and kill, and a fierce storm grounds the *Aurora* on the very island that Kate's grandfather spoke about—which proves to be the pirates' secret hideaway. This detailed and dramatic journey from a master storyteller reads like a classic high adventure novel.

How have your most challenging moments shaped you into who you are today?

The Field Guide to the North American Teenager

BEN PHILIPPE

For Norris Kaplan, Austin, Texas—location of his mother's new professor gig—is the antithesis of his true home in Montreal, Canada. Gone are hockey hooligans and routinely spoken French, replaced by relentless heat and the ubiquitous orange of the UT Longhorns. Compounding these differences is the fact that Norris is a Black Haitian Canadian kid stuck in cowboy country. He resolves to build a barrier of snark to keep everyone out until he can get back north, where he hopes to reunite with his estranged father. However, Norris doesn't count on falling head over heels for the devilishly mysterious, soulful, and fiery Aarti Puri.

Describe a time when you pretended to be someone or something you were not. What happened?

Nation

TERRY PRATCHETT

"Somewhere in the South Pelagic Ocean," a tidal wave wipes out the population of a small island—except for Mau, who was paddling his dugout canoe home after a month spent alone, preparing to become a man. The wave also sweeps a sailing ship carrying Daphne, an English girl, up onto the island and deposits it in the rain forest, where Mau finds her. Over the months that follow, they learn to communicate while welcoming more people to their shores and building a community of survivors. Mau searches for the meaning behind his people's gods, while Daphne applies her nineteenth-century knowledge of science and history to the many puzzles she discovers in this unfamiliar place.

If you were stranded on a desert island, what three things would you want with you?

52 YA Books Every Book Lover Should Read

Long Way Down

JASON REYNOLDS

This story takes place in the span of one minute and seven seconds. First, fifteen-year-old Will Holloman sets the scene by relating his brother Shawn's murder two days prior—gunned down while buying soap for their mother. Next, he lays out The Rules: don't cry, don't snitch, always get revenge. Now that the reader is up to speed, Will tucks Shawn's gun into his waistband and steps into an elevator, steeled to execute rule number three and shoot his brother's killer. Yet, the simple seven-floor descent becomes a revelatory trip. At each floor, the doors open to admit someone killed by the same cycle of violence that Will's about to enter. He's properly freaked out, but as the seconds tick by and floors count down, each new occupant drops some knowledge and pushes Will to examine his plans for that gun.

Describe a choice you regret. What were the circumstances?

_____

_____

_____

_____

52 YA Books Every Book Lover Should Read

How I Live Now

MEG ROSOFF

A fifteen-year-old contemporary urbanite named Daisy, sent to England to summer with relatives, falls in love with her aunt's "oldy worldy" farm and her soulful cousins—especially Edmond, with whom she forms "the world's most inappropriate case of sexual obsession." Matters veer in a startling direction when terrorists strike while Daisy's aunt is out of the country, war erupts, and soldiers divide the cousins by gender between two guardians. Determined to rejoin Edmond, Daisy and her youngest cousin embark upon a dangerous journey that brings them face-to-face with horrific violence and undreamt-of deprivation. Set in roughly the present day, this harrowing, alternate-reality exploration of a potential third world war is somber, strange, and evocative.

What one goal are you determined to achieve?

41

Bone Gap

LAURA RUBY

For all appearances, Bone Gap is a sluggish farming town that most people want to escape, a place "with gaps just wide enough for people to slip away...leaving only their stories behind." That's what folks assume happened when Roza disappeared from the state fair, but seventeen-year-old Finn knows better. He's the only one who sees her leave, but his description of her abductor—that he moves like a shivering cornstalk—doesn't help the police, and the people of Bone Gap resentfully believe that Finn helped the beloved girl disappear because she wanted to. Her departure drives a wedge between Finn and his brother Sean—Finn feels like Sean isn't doing enough to look for her, and Sean thinks Finn is hiding something about the night she left. The gaps in Bone are "gaps in the world. In the space of things." Those gaps in the town are loose enough that a person can fall clear through to the other side of reality, and that's precisely where the cornstalk man took Roza and where Finn must go to rescue her.

What do you see that other people miss?

52 YA Books Every Book Lover Should Read

42

Scythe

NEAL SHUSTERMAN

In the year 2042, humans conquered death. Now, in the postmortal society of MidMerica, people can live for millennia, either reanimated from fatal accidents or "turning the corner" when they get old by resetting themselves to a younger age. But Earth remains the only habitable planet and so exist the Scythes, tasked with keeping the population in check: those who a Scythe gleans stay dead. Citra and Rowan are two teenagers in this world, chosen to apprentice the Honorable Scythe Faraday. Neither teen wants to learn the ways of a Scythe, and neither wants to begin gleaning lives, although Faraday tells them that, actually, only the uneager have any business accepting the mantle of a Scythe. Citra and Rowan begin their year-long apprenticeships both as allies and competitors, as only one will be given the dubious prize of Scythedom, and they face increasingly higher stakes as they race toward the end of their apprenticeship.

What would it be like to have the power of life and death over someone?

DATE STARTED:

DATE FINISHED:

MY RATING:

☆ ☆ ☆ ☆ ☆

52 YA Books Every Book Lover Should Read

43

Midwinterblood

MARCUS SEDGWICK

In the year 2073, a reporter named Eric is sent to Blessed Island to research a rare flower called the Dragon Orchid. There he finds an insular community of mysterious villagers, a delicious tea that has him losing days at a time, and a beguiling girl named Merle. Flashback to 2011. An archaeologist is digging on Blessed Island, where he meets a quiet boy named Eric and his mother, Merle. This story, written in reverse, centers on two characters whose identities shift as they are reborn throughout the ages. There is a stranded World War II pilot, a painter trying to resurrect his career in 1901, two children being told a ghost story in 1848, and more, all the way back to a king and queen in a "Time Unknown." Part love story, part mystery, part horror, this story's strange spell will capture you.

If you could travel back in time, to what time period would you go? What would you do there? If you could travel into the future, what would you hope to see?

DATE STARTED:

DATE FINISHED:

MY RATING:

☆ ☆ ☆ ☆ ☆

52 YA Books Every Book Lover Should Read

The Scorpio Races

MAGGIE STIEFVATER

Though Thisby, an island near Britain, has cars and electricity, it is nevertheless fantastical; it's home to a fierce breed of water horses, the capaill uisce, man eaters who rise from the autumn seas to terrorize the islanders. They can be captured and somewhat tamed, however, and once a year the island hosts the Scorpio Races, a beachside contest that draws tourists but is often fatal to the riders. Sean Kendrick is one of those racers, a four-time champion on his dangerous but still faithful steed. Kate "Puck" Connolly is new to the races and the first woman rider. Due to a loophole in the rules, Kate is riding a regular horse, her beloved Dove, who she trusts to run true against the more frightening contestants. Both riders have deeper personal motives for wanting to win.

What contest would you like to win? How would you defeat the competition?

Laura Dean Keeps Breaking Up with Me

MARIKO TAMAKI, ILLUSTRATED BY ROSEMARY VALERO-O'CONNELL

Freddy finds herself in an on-again, off-again relationship with the impossibly cool Laura Dean, who, surely not by accident, has an air of James Dean about her, from her floppy hair to her slouchy posture to her piercing gaze. Freddy feels invincible in Laura's orbit, and even after things truly go wrong, like when Laura sneaks off to make out with other girls, Freddy is inexorably lured back in. Freddy's friends range from dismayed to resigned, but none so much as Doodle, who's dealing with problems of their own and desperately needs a friend. Compulsively readable and heartbreakingly true, this graphic novel goes straight to the heart of why it's so difficult to get out of a toxic relationship.

How would your friends describe you?

52 YA Books Every Book Lover Should Read

Strange the Dreamer

LAINI TAYLOR

Lazlo Strange, an orphaned infant who grew up to be a librarian, has had a quiet first two decades of life. But Lazlo, reader of fairy tales, longs to learn more about a distant, nearly mythical city called Weep after its true name was stolen. When a group of warriors from that very place come seeking help, Lazlo, never before a man of action, may actually see his dream fulfilled. Weep, though, is a city still reeling from the aftermath of a brutal war, and hidden there is a girl named Sarai and her four companions, all of whom have singular talents and devastating secrets.

What do you dream of doing in your future? Where do you dream of going?

The Hate U Give

ANGIE THOMAS

Sixteen-year-old Starr lives in two very different worlds: one is her home in a poor Black urban neighborhood, the other is the tony suburban prep school she attends and the white boy she dates there. Her bifurcated life changes dramatically when she is the only witness to the unprovoked police shooting of her unarmed friend Khalil and is challenged to speak out—though with trepidation—about the injustices being done in the event's wake. As the case becomes national news, violence erupts in her neighborhood, and Starr finds herself and her family caught in the middle. Difficulties are exacerbated by their encounters with the local drug lord for whom Khalil was dealing to earn money for his impoverished family. If there is to be hope for change, Starr comes to realize, it must be through the exercise of her voice, even if it puts her and her family in harm's way.

How can you use your voice to promote social justice?

Piecing Me Together

RENÉE WATSON

"Who owns the river and the line, and the hook, and the worm?" wonders Jade, a scholarship kid at Portland's prestigious St. Francis High. Through her first two years of school, she's had to balance her home life in a poor neighborhood with her life at a school populated mostly by rich white kids. When offered a mentorship for at-risk girls (which includes a full college scholarship), she jumps at the opportunity to learn how to be a successful Black woman. However, she soon suspects that her mentor, Maxine, may only have a superficial understanding of Jade's challenges and that there may be things Jade can teach her.

What parts of yourself do you limit or hide in order to fit in?

52 YA Books Every Book Lover Should Read

52 YA Books Every Book Lover Should Read

American Born Chinese

GENE LUEN YANG, ILLUSTRATED BY THE AUTHOR

With vibrant colors and visual panache, this graphic novel focuses on three characters in tales that touch on facets of Chinese American life. Jin is a boy faced with the casual racism of fellow students and the pressure of his crush on a Caucasian girl; the Monkey King, a character from Chinese folklore, has attained great power but feels he is being held back because of what the gods perceive as his lowly status; and Danny, a popular high school student, suffers through an annual visit from his cousin Chin-Kee, a walking, talking compendium of exaggerated Chinese stereotypes. Each of the characters is flawed but familiar, and all share a deep, unforeseen connection.

Describe a time when you tried to be someone or something you are not. What was the result?

The Sun Is Also a Star

NICOLA YOON

On a summer morning in New York City, Daniel and Natasha wake up as strangers. This is a day that could catapult their lives into entirely new directions that neither of them wants to take. Natasha has only hours left to prevent her family's deportation to Jamaica after a minor legal infraction jeopardizes their stay in the United States. Daniel dreads sealing his fate with an alumni interview that will pave his way to a career in medicine, as his Korean family expects. Despite a day packed with Natasha's desperate race against time and a tangled system, and Daniel's difficult tug-of-war between familial pressures and autonomy, love finds a way in, takes hold, and changes them both forever.

Do you believe in love at first sight? Why or why not?

51

American Street

IBI ZOBOI

Fabiola Toussaint is a Haitian teen adjusting to her new life in Detroit. Fabiola's dream of a better life with her aunt and cousins in America snags when her mother is detained at the U.S. border. Forced to continue alone, she must also confront the reality that her new neighborhood is every bit as dangerous as the one she left behind in Port-au-Prince. Drugs, gangs, and violence pervade the status quo, but thanks to her cousins' tough reputations, Fabiola can find her footing. Tender moments offset the dangerous realities and the girls' struggles for survival, and the complexities of the characters make this a fierce and beautiful story.

What is the bravest thing you have ever done?

The Book Thief

MARKUS ZUSAK

Death is the narrator of this lengthy, powerful story of a town in Nazi Germany. He is a kindly, caring Death, overwhelmed by the souls he has to collect from people in the gas chambers, from soldiers on the battlefields, and from civilians killed in bombings. Death focuses on a young orphan, Liesel; her loving foster parents; the Jewish fugitive they are hiding; and a wild but gentle teen neighbor, Rudy, who defies the Hitler Youth and convinces Liesel to steal for fun. After Liesel learns to read, she steals books from everywhere. When she reads a book in the bomb shelter, even a Nazi woman is enthralled. Then the book thief writes her own story.

Describe the impact a particular book has had on your life.

ABOUT THE AMERICAN LIBRARY ASSOCIATION

The American Library Association (ALA) is the trusted voice of libraries and the national organization that provides resources to inspire library and information workers to transform their communities through essential programs and services. The association is committed to using a social justice framework in its work, with key areas including advocacy for libraries and for the profession, diversity, education and lifelong learning, equitable access to information and library services for all, intellectual freedom, literacy, sustainability, and the transformation of libraries.

The reviews in this book come from *Booklist*, the book review magazine of the American Library Association and an invaluable source of reading recommendations for all readers. *Booklist* is an essential collection development and readers' advisory tool for thousands of librarians. For more information, visit booklistonline.com.

Learn more about how you can stay connected to what's going on in libraries and how you can help advocate for your own library at ilovelibraries.org.